PIRATES AROUND THE WORLD

Terror on the High Seas

Black Bart
(Bartholomew Roberts)

John Bankston

Mitchell Lane
PUBLISHERS

P.O. Box 196
Hockessin, DE 19707
www.mitchelllane.com

Mitchell Lane
PUBLISHERS

Printing   1   2   3   4   5   6   7   8

Anne Bonny
Black Bart (Bartholomew Roberts)
Blackbeard (Edward Teach)
François L'Olonnais

Long Ben (Henry Every)
Sir Francis Drake
Sir Henry Morgan
William Kidd

Library of Congress Cataloging-in-Publication Data
Bankston, John, 1974–
 Black Bart (Bartholomew Roberts) / by John Bankston.
    pages cm. — (Pirates around the world: terror on the high seas)
Includes bibliographical references and index.
ISBN 978-1-68020-038-6 (library bound)
1. Roberts, Bartholomew, 1682?-1722—Juvenile literature.
2. Pirates—Biography—Juvenile literature. I. Title.
G537.R74B34 2015
910.4'5—dc23
[B]
                                                     2015003192

eBook ISBN: 978-1-68020-039-3

Contents

Words in **bold** throughout can be found in the Glossary.

This traditional image of Bartholomew "Black Bart" Roberts appeared in a well-known book on pirates. No one really knows what Roberts looked like or exactly how he dressed.

Death of a Pirate

The pirates had spent the day having a good time on Prince's Island, off the coast of West Africa. They were enjoying the warm beach when the militia opened fire. Their ship, the *Royal Rover*, was anchored nearby. Unfortunately, the island's governor had learned about their plans to kidnap him. He ordered the attack. The pirates were unprepared.

The *Rover*'s captain, Howell Davis, was shot four times. He stumbled toward the shoreline. For a moment, he could see the ship he had commanded. Then a fifth shot ended his life. The pirates who had been with him were officers. Now most of them were dead, wounded or destined for jail. The *Royal Rover* needed a new leader.

The *Royal Rover* sailed in the early 1700s. It was a time when most countries were ruled by kings and queens. The United States was not yet an independent country. The Thirteen Colonies in North America were still ruled by England, and Americans had little to say about how they were governed. During that time, captains of merchant vessels were free to inflict brutal punishments on their crews, who often went unpaid. During those days, sailors could do little to defend themselves from being treated poorly.

On most ships, captains lived in luxury. The men they commanded endured cramped holds or slept on deck. In contrast, on pirate ships, no one—not even the captain—had

dibs on where to sleep. On most ships, the captain earned much more than his men. On pirate ships, the crew received one share of any "purchase," their term for the goods they seized. The captain got just one extra share.

Pirate ships were **democratic**. Every pirate had a vote. With Davis dead, the *Royal Rover*'s crew needed to elect a captain. Otherwise, no one would decide where to go next or whether to attack the men who had killed Davis.

Pirate elections were usually held in steerage, on the lowest deck of the ship. While they discussed who could lead them, the pirates drank a rum punch made from alcohol, limes and sugar.

Captains decided their ship's destination. A wise choice meant riches for the crew. A poor choice meant dying of thirst or starvation on the open water. When a pirate ship was captured, the captain was usually the first to perish.

The pirates on board the *Royal Rover* could have elected one of the "Lords." Lords were experienced pirates. They knew how to fight and how to lead. One of the top choices was Walter Kennedy. Although he was only 24 years old, he had spent years **plundering** and fighting. One of two survivors of the beach attack, he was considered brutal and impulsive.

Kennedy and other experienced crewmen were passed over. Instead, the pirates chose a newcomer. John "Bartholomew" Roberts was in his late thirties. He had been captured from a merchant ship just six weeks earlier.

Roberts had spent his adult life on board ships. In his twenties, he probably served in the Royal Navy, fighting for England during wartime. Roberts was elected captain in July 1721. One of his first decisions was to leave Africa.

The attack against Captain Howell Davis was brutal and unexpected. His death meant another pirate would be elected to be the leader.

New Destinations

Like other eighteenth century sailing ships, the *Royal Rover* was controlled by trade winds. Trade winds blow in different directions, depending on their location and the time of year. These winds sped the *Royal Rover* across the Atlantic Ocean.

As the *Royal Rover* sailed to South America, the pirates knew the risks. They hoped trusting their new captain would bring rewards.

The trip was quite fast for the time. It took less than a month for the *Royal Rover* to reach Ferdando de Noronha, an island 200 miles from Brazil. This was the only bit of luck the men enjoyed. They'd traveled over 4,000 miles without

a decent purchase. Supplies were scarce. Their water was almost gone.

Unfortunately, it was the dry season. The entire crew of over 100 men survived for weeks on fewer than 700 gallons of fresh water. For food, the men ate pork preserved with salt. The salt kept the meat from spoiling. It also made the men even thirstier.

As the pirates began to take ill, Roberts had to take bold action. He ordered the ship to sail toward Brazil, the world's leading producer of gold. Every day, ships left her harbors for Europe filled with the precious metal.

"Upon this coast our rovers cruised for about nine weeks, keeping generally out of sight of land but without seeing a sail," Charles Johnson wrote in *A General History of the Robberies and Murders of the Most Notorious Pyrates* in 1724. Although they went ashore to get more supplies, as Johnson reported, not seeing another ship "discouraged them so that they determined to . . . steer for the West Indies."[1]

The *Royal Rover* was near the eastern edge of Brazil when the first ship appeared. On the open water, a ship's sails are visible for miles—long before the rest of the boat comes into view. The men were excited. Then they saw another sail, and then yet another. Soon there were almost too many ships to count.

Roberts had stumbled onto a 40-ship convoy. This line of ships was headed back to Portugal, their home country. The ships were certain to be heavy with treasure. They were also protected by Man-of-Wars, large naval ships loaded with guns.

The *Royal Rover*'s new captain decided to take his chances. If he succeeded, the pirates could all be very rich. If he failed, Roberts and his men faced certain death.

A General History

No one knows exactly what John "Bartholomew" Roberts looked like. He was tall, which was rare for someone who had grown up poor in seventeenth century England. Poor people often went hungry. Because they did not have enough to eat as children, most adults were usually several inches shorter than rich people.

People who met Roberts also described him as fairly heavy and dark skinned. They also remembered one other detail about the pirate captain. Like the pirates in stories, Roberts dressed very well.

Newspapers described Roberts as a brutal killer. They did this to attract more readers, not because it was true. Although he did many horrible deeds, he did not hurt or kill as often as they claimed.

Much of what we know about Roberts comes from a best-selling book written by Captain Charles Johnson. Published in 1724, Johnson's *A General History of the Robberies and Murders of the Most Notorious Pyrates* described the life and crimes of well-known sea thieves like Edward "Blackbeard" Teach and John "Bartholomew" Roberts. Johnson also wrote about two famous female pirates, Mary Read and Anne Bonny.

In the early 1900s, Claud Lovat Fraser wrote a foreword for a different version of Johnson's book, called simply *Pirates*. As Fraser explained, the book "has the merit of being written, if not by a Pirate, at least by one who came into actual contact with them."[2]

Nearly three hundred years later, respected biographers quote Johnson's descriptions of Roberts' life. Despite the writer's success, his identity is a mystery. Many believed he was really *Robinson Crusoe* author Daniel Defoe, although this has not been proven.

This illustration of a 1905 oil painting shows "The Buccaneer," a sixteenth-century pirate. Often dressed in whatever he could steal, some pirates enjoyed nicer clothing than most sailors.

Life at Sea

The war was waged on land and sea. The attacker's boats were faster, their weapons stronger. To the victims, they were the "Sea People." Today we know them as the first organized pirate group.

The earliest history of piracy dates back to the time soon after people first launched crude boats into the water. Some used boats to fish and trade goods. Others used them to steal.

Over three thousand years ago, the Sea People attacked countries by their coastlines along the eastern Mediterranean. They invaded Egypt and conquered Greece. Powerful **empires** eventually used ships for fighting and protection, but these early navies did not end piracy. It remained a problem along trade routes, the well-known courses along which merchant vessels traveled.

In the 1600s, French settlers in the Caribbean were driven from their homes by the Spanish. They moved to the islands that later became Haiti, the Dominican Republic and Jamaica. There they survived by catching and killing wild animals. The meat smoker they used for cooking was called a *buccan*. They were known as **buccaneers**.

By the 1640s, buccaneers were attacking Spanish **galleons**. Under the cover of darkness, buccaneers in tiny boats slipped beside the large, square-rigged ships. They boarded before an alarm was raised. Well-armed and ruthless, buccaneers were aided by the English. That support ended with the treaty between England and Spain in 1670.

In the decades afterward, France, Spain and England fought a series of wars. Men who might have become pirates instead became privateers. Privateers carried an agreement they had signed with their home country. They could attack ships from warring countries and keep the cargo. Countries like England benefited. They received a portion of the stolen cargo. The attacks also disrupted supply lines. Some privateers became rich. A few even became famous.

In the early 1700s, the European nations were at peace. Men who had been in the navy were out of work. Privateering had become illegal. And merchant ships weren't hiring very many crewmen.

Talented and idle, sailors often turned to piracy. The waters near the New World of North and South America were filled with pirates. Pirates also attacked the coastlines of Africa and India. With so many pirates robbing ships during the years 1690 to 1720 (approximately), the period was called "The Golden Age of Piracy."

A Pirate's Beginnings

Just a few years earlier, around 1682, the man who would be called "Black Bart" was born. John Roberts grew up in a rural corner of southwestern England called Wales. Wales was once a separate country from England, and people who grew up in Wales spoke Welsh rather than English. Most made their living raising cattle or mining coal. The port towns of Wales, such as Fishguard, Haverfordwest and Cardiff, provided a steady supply of sailors. They were also the habitats of many pirates.

Bartholomew Roberts' hometown of Little Newcastle was a damp and desperately poor place with few opportunities.

Roberts was slightly better off than most because his father was a fairly successful rancher. Unfortunately, English law kept him from dividing his herd among his sons. After he died, the oldest received the ranch and the cattle. Young John Roberts received nothing.

Very little is known about Roberts before he became a pirate. He learned to read and write—a rare skill for anyone who wasn't born rich in the 1600s. He may have learned at home, at school or even as an apprentice. Apprentice sailors began working on boats in their early teens. It was an even more dangerous challenge for a youth than it would be for an adult. Still, for many, it was a path to becoming an officer. Officers on ships commanded the crew and were better paid.

The War of the Grand Alliance began while Roberts was a teenager. Lasting from 1689 to 1697, the war involved England and other European countries which fought the French efforts to expand. Four years later, during the War of Spanish Succession, England again joined other European powers against France. Because of his youthful age, Roberts most likely spent time in the British Royal Navy during those wars. Although his war record is long gone, he probably learned to fight the way most pirates did—by serving in the military.

After the wars, Roberts was lucky enough to find work. His life on board a merchant ship was difficult. Ships used a four-hour watch system. Sailors worked and kept an eye out for pirates for four hours. Then they took four hours to rest before returning to work. Never being able to sleep for more than four hours in a row made for some very tired sailors!

Roberts' name appears as a mate, or junior officer, on the crew list of a sloop from Barbados. Sloops were smaller

The late 1600s and early 1700s were marked by a series of European wars. Here a painting depicts the "Sea Battle of Vigo Bay," which was fought in October of 1702 during the War of the Spanish Succession.

and faster than most sailing vessels. Pirates who made their base around the Caribbean preferred sloops for their speed. Despite his experience with sloops, Roberts chose larger, heavier vessels.

Larger ships were built for ocean crossings. They weren't fast but they could hold more cannons—which were usually called guns onboard a ship. These large weapons fired everything from metal balls to chains and nails. They were incredibly destructive, taking down both men and rigging (which supported the sails and masts on a ship).

Roberts moved up in command, becoming a third mate onboard the *Princess,* one of many merchant ships traveling between Europe and the New World. The *Princess,* like many European ships, also traveled to Africa. In June 1719, she anchored off the continent's Gold Coast and was loaded with human cargo—slaves.

The Slave Trade

As European countries such as Spain, Portugal and England colonized the Americas, they used slave labor to cultivate **plantations** and mines. African slaves were captured by other Africans in the continent's interior sections. They were then brought to the coastlines. Stripped and chained on shore, they were transported in small boats to European ships anchored nearby.

Life on board a slave ship was brutal. Men, women and children were kept in the ship's hold in cramped conditions. They received very little food or water. They spent most of their time unable to move. Many died from starvation, disease or just despair.

The horrors slaves endured are well known. Less well known are the conditions endured by the average sailor. Sailors were whipped or chained for minor infractions. They did not eat well. They earned very little money. Many of them never lived long enough to spend their meager pay.

On average, at least one of every eight slaves bound for North America died in transit. Slavers traveled from Europe to Africa and back, so they spent a far greater amount of time on ships. Their death rate was also higher—one out of five. So, on a single round trip journey, twenty of every one hundred slavers died.

Unlike most sailors, pirates were safe from scurvy. This disease affected anyone at sea for over a month. Because back then ships could not stock fresh fruits and vegetables, people onboard did not get enough vitamin C. This caused scurvy. Their gums bled. Wounds wouldn't heal. Eventually some even died. Although the pirates didn't know this, the vitamin C found in the limes they used in rum punch protected them from scurvy.

For sailors docked off the coast of Africa, a mosquito bite could be deadly. The victim of a bite by a malarial mosquito suffered an illness like the flu. It got worse and worse. In the 1700s, many Europeans who went to Africa died of malaria—sometimes half the people on board a ship. Docked off the coast of Africa, Roberts was probably more worried about malaria than pirates.

A Tricky Pirate

While Roberts endured life onboard a merchant vessel, Howell Davis was beginning his career as a pirate. Davis also grew up in Wales. In 1718, Davis was onboard a merchant ship—the *Cadogan*—when it was attacked by pirates. Seized along with a number of his comrades, Davis quickly took to the pirate life. He enjoyed the adventure, the drinking and pursuing women at every port of call.

As a pirate captain, he preferred deception to warfare. Pirate ships were often not as well-armed or crewed as the ships they attacked. Brute force did not assure victory. Besides, sending round after round of cannon fire into a merchant ship risked destroying valuable cargo.

Pirate captains needed to be crafty. Davis was one of the craftiest. Davis usually seized ships without firing a single shot. He fooled ship captains into thinking he commanded another merchant vessel. Other times he pretended to be better armed. Once he kidnapped a governor who thought Davis was a legal privateer. To Davis, the ships anchored off the West African coast on that June day in 1719 were just one more chance at "purchase." He didn't realize he was about to change John Roberts' life forever.

High Fashion on the High Seas

From Errol Flynn's Captain Blood to Johnny Depp's Jack Sparrow, movie stars have gained millions of fans playing pirates. On screen pirates usually wear head scarves and large, hoop earrings. They might sport tri-cornered hats decorated by a skull-and-crossbones. In fact, the skull-and-crossbones appears all over pirate's clothing in the movies.

When people imagine the appearance of pirates, they aren't picturing how pirates in the early 1700s really looked. Instead, the pirates they imagine, along with the look of most pirates on screen, are based on drawings made by Howard Pyle.

The "Golden Age of Piracy" dates more than a century before photography. Pirates did not pose for portraits. Famous pirates probably looked nothing like they do in drawings. Instead, artists like Pyle used their imaginations. When Pyle began drawing pirates in the late 1800s, he drew them dressed like people who were then called "gypsies." Pyle believed the people today called "Romani" were the perfect models for pirates. Both pirates and gypsies traveled all over the world without a fixed home. So he dressed his pirates like gypsies, with headscarves and gold earrings.

Pirates in the early 1700s dressed much like other sailors. They wore short, knit caps, and shirts with narrow-band collars and sleeves. They might also display a well-made waist coat or leather trousers plundered from a ship. And the skull and cross bones did not decorate anything onboard the ship other than the skull and cross bones flag.

John "Bartholomew" Roberts stood out. Many who saw him claimed he was always well dressed. Indeed, in his final battle, author Charles Johnson claims Roberts wore, "a rich crimson damask [red patterned] waist coat and breeches, a red feather in his hat, a gold chain round his neck with a diamond cross hanging to it, a sword in his hand and two pair of pistols, hanging at the end of a silk sling flung over his shoulders."[1]

With his frilly waist coat, tricorn hat and knee length trousers, the pirate in this engraving is wearing the style of the time— or whatever he can steal. Bartholomew Roberts is believed to have dressed quite well.

The Reluctant Pirate

Sharks circled the *Princess*. The creatures fed off of the unlucky and the scared. They made a meal of slaves trying to escape. They also fed on sailors who fell overboard and African traders who took a misstep. Perhaps as John Roberts stared out into the Atlantic Ocean, he sensed even deadlier prey approaching.

The *Princess* was a large, ocean-going vessel. Weighing some 140 tons and running 85 feet long, it was no still match for the danger approaching from the west.

It was a little after noon, on June 6, 1719, when the pirates arrived. At first, Roberts and other crewmen thought the two ships were slavers—except the pair of approaching ships seemed too fast and well-armed to be merchant vessels. As they drew closer, Roberts noticed the large number of crew on deck. Every one of them was armed and waiting. Any questions he had were answered when they raised a black flag. Roberts suddenly realized who faced them: pirates.

The African slave traders fled in canoes. Onshore, the British Royal African Company's fort was nearly two miles away. Its cannons were out of range. Outnumbered and outgunned, the captain of the *Princess* stood down.

The merchant ship's second mate, John Stephenson, joined a few others in a longboat. Then they rowed to the pirate ship. Stephenson's job was to give up as little as possible while keeping the *Princess* and her crew safe.

The pirates were given silver, food and fine clothing. They soon left the harbor with a different sort of treasure—34 new crew members. As Stephenson later explained, Davis "asked which of them would enter with him and told them that he would make a gentleman of them all."[1]

In earlier centuries, pirates wore armor for protection. Instead, Davis's pirates wore the finest stolen clothing. They looked a cut above the average sailor (and slavers were considered the lowest class of all).

One after another, the new arrivals swore a pirate oath. Only one refused. Unlike the others, he did not want to be a pirate. He asked to go back to the *Princess*. He was an officer. He had little interest in joining this unruly, drunken gang of thieves.

Davis didn't care. This disciplined, sober man was just what the unruly drunken gang of thieves needed. But even Davis couldn't know Roberts would soon be captaining his ship.

Roberts Takes Charge

The *Royal Rover* continued to sail along the African coast. Over several weeks, Roberts began to see how different it was to crew a pirate ship. Because pirate ships had many more men, each did less work. There was no four-hour watch system. And when a ship wore out, they just stole a new one.

By now, the *Royal Rover* carried more than stolen cargo. There were a number of slaves as well. Pirates often sold the slaves, but sometimes the men wound up working as crew. Although they weren't paid, they were sometimes given their freedom.

One slave decided not to wait. He had overheard Davis discussing plans to kidnap a governor and hold him for ransom. While they anchored off Prince's Island, the slave swam ashore, eluding both pirates and sharks. When he told the governor about Davis's plans, the slave sealed the pirate's fate.

Davis's death meant a vote for a new captain. One pirate spoke in Roberts' favor, saying, ". . . it is my advice . . . we pitch upon a man of courage, and skilled in navigation; one who by his counsel and bravery seems best able to defend this [ship and her crew] and ward us from the dangers. . . ." The pirates agreed. Roberts became the new captain.[2]

His first job was revenge. Davis had been well liked. The governor, the militia, indeed the whole of Prince's Island, needed to pay for his death. According to author Charles

Although the picture shows a slave ship from the 1860s, the cramped and miserable conditions would have been familiar to Captain Roberts, who crewed on slave ships in the 1700s.

Johnson, 30 pirates led by Walter Kennedy attacked the fort and set fire to it before throwing its cannons into the ocean. They even wanted to attack the town, but Roberts convinced them it was too dangerous.

A few people who lived near the fort at the time claimed there was no such attack. Instead, the men fired their guns at the town before sailing away toward Brazil. The men were too busy dreaming of the gold being shipped from South America to take the chance of attacking a well-armed fort.

After crossing the Atlantic, the new captain of the *Royal Rover* didn't just find one ship. He found forty.

Treasure!

Roberts was crafty. Like a lion stalking his prey, he hung back, waiting for the slowest ship. Then, like the king of the beasts taking down a gazelle, Roberts ordered the *Royal Rover* to move in. As the ship approached, he ordered his men to raise the French flag. Then Roberts pretended to be the captain of a European merchant ship.

The other ship's captain believed him. He slowed down. By the time he realized what was really happening, it was too late.

Roberts climbed aboard. He wasn't interested in this small ship with its tiny cargo. He wanted a real prize. To get it, he pumped the captain for information. If the captain pointed out the vessel with the most gold, Roberts would let him go. Otherwise, death was certain.

The captain told Roberts the *Sagrada Familia* held the most wealth. Unfortunately, it also held the most large guns—40 compared to the 32 Roberts commanded. Although the *Rover* held 200 men, the *Sagrada* held one hundred and fifty. It would be a bloody battle if the *Sagrada* resisted.

Since the ruse had worked once, Roberts tried it again. This time he was not as lucky. Although the ship's captain promised to come over, it soon looked more as though the men were getting ready for a fight. Roberts did not hesitate. He ordered his crew to fire a "broadside"—that is, to fire all the guns from the side of the ship. The ship's gun ports were opened and over a dozen cannons erupted. Cannon balls exploded across the *Sagrada Familia*'s deck—tearing apart both rigging and men. In the thick smoke, pirates swung grappling hooks from the *Rover* to the *Sagrada*. They then used them to pull themselves onto the ship. There are many,

The guns mounted on ships (called cannons on land) were brutally destructive weapons of war. Fired at close range, they could wreck a ship and rip people apart.

many ways for a pirate to die. Being flattened between two ships is one of the worst.

Still, according to Johnson, only two pirates died. The Portuguese lost many more lives.

Victory provided an unexpected fortune. The cargo included 40,000 gold moidores, or coins, worth over $100,000 at the time. Divided among the crew, it meant each man would receive more than $500. In the early 1700s, this was more than most sailors earned in their entire life.

The success meant Roberts had proven his talents as a captain. After docking in Cayenne on the northeastern coast of South America, his men celebrated as only pirates can. They drank huge amounts of rum punch and enjoyed the attentions of local women. Roberts did not drink. He also did not pursue women. Instead, he stayed on board the ship, drinking tea, reading and perhaps looking at the stars. During his first night as a successful pirate, he probably imagined how he would spend all his money.

He never had a chance to enjoy his riches. Just days later, Roberts captained a captured sloop, hoping to overtake another ship. He failed. Roberts had put Kennedy in charge of the *Royal Rover*, along with the captured wealth, and had left them behind him.

For over a week, Roberts and his men fought unfavorable winds as they struggled to return to the place where they'd left the *Rover*. During this time, they suffered from lack of food and water. When Roberts returned, the *Rover* was gone. So was Kennedy and 40 other crew members. Worst of all, Kennedy had taken with him all of the gold and other treasures from the *Sagrada*.

Roberts and his crew were once again broke. Their supplies were low. And it looked as though his career as a pirate captain would end as quickly as it had begun.

The Articles of
John Bartholomew Roberts

John Roberts became almost as well known for the pledges he made his pirates sign as for the ships he attacked. These "articles," that is, the terms that would govern the ship, included both promises for the pirates and punishments for misbehavior.

Many books describing the pirates of the 1700s question how truly democratic the ships were. Roberts clearly was in command. As he gained successes, he was able to tell the others where they should set sail and which ships they would attack. This was, in many ways, a sign of the trust he had established among the pirates, rather than a sign that he was controlling them. After all, if the pirates did not want to go along with Roberts, it would be a simple matter to vote him out as the captain.

The crew had to agree to the articles. According to Johnson, and several pirates from the crew, Roberts' first article was: "Every man had a vote in affairs of moment." The articles also ordered that both rum and food be distributed equally." Not telling fellow pirates about cargo could lead to marooning—leaving a pirate to die on a **deserted** island. Robbing a fellow pirate was punished by cutting the criminal's nose and ears.[3]

Roberts also tried to control his pirates' drinking by giving them an early bedtime. In the articles, it was ordered that "The lights and candles to be put out at eight o'clock at night. If any of the crew after that hour still remained inclined to drinking, they were to do it on the open deck." Roberts' articles also forbade gambling for money and did not allow women or boys onto the ship.[4]

Two of Bartholomew Roberts' ships sail off the coast of Guinea. The Royal Fortune and the Ranger are shown flying the flag he had specially designed. As Roberts' fearsome reputation grew, merchant ships often surrendered at the sight of his flag.

Some Good Plunders

By the time the pirates reached the Caribbean, they had a new ship and a new captain. Now on board the *Good Fortune*, the crew had voted to remove Bartholomew Roberts as their leader. In his place, they put one of the men who had been passed over at Prince's Island, Thomas Anstis.

For a while, the pirates were lucky. The waters around Barbados were filled with merchant ships. Attacking them was relatively easy. This was because of the way ships stayed on course, or **navigated** themselves.

Captains set their course by measuring the angle of the sun at noon. This gave them their ship's north-south position or latitude. Latitude measures the north-south distance from the equator in degrees. To reach Barbados, captains determined the line for 13 degrees north and stayed on it as they sailed across the Atlantic. The pirates knew this. All they had to do was lie in wait along the same line. A merchant ship was sure to appear.

For the new captain, the method was almost foolproof. For several months, they plundered without pause. Their actions did not go unnoticed.

Although the Royal Navy regularly patrolled the waters along the Caribbean, their numbers had been reduced by a dispute. The governor of Barbados, Robert Lowther, sent two naval captains to jail when they refused to turn over the cargo of a captured pirate ship. Local merchants, fed up

with pirate attacks, convinced Lowther to let them take care of the problem. He granted them naval powers, outfitting two merchant ships with guns and men.

On February 26, 1720, the *Good Fortune* was spotted. The two merchant ships, *Somerset Galley* and the *Phillipa*, were ready. The *Good Fortune's* new captain thought he'd found another ship rich with purchase. He was not as interested in the crafty tactics used by Roberts and Davis. Instead, he ordered his men to immediately fire a broadside across the *Somerset's* bow. But instead of giving up, the merchant vessel opened fire.

It was a bloodbath. Pirates in a longboat were killed, as were many of the men on board the *Good Fortune*. Those who survived were saved only by the poor steering of the *Phillipa*. The ship cut between the two fighting vessels, forcing the *Somerset* to still her cannons. The *Good Fortune* lived up to her name.

Roberts Returns

Roberts retook command. For several months, not a single ship reported being attacked by the pirate or his crew. In June, they sailed north—all the way to Canada and Newfoundland. Newfoundland, an island on the northeast coast of Canada, was a world away from the Caribbean. Cold and primitive, it offered Roberts and his men ample opportunities for plunder.

While fishing ships carried less cargo than the ships his crew had raided further south, there were many more of those shipping vessels, and they were unprotected. Unlike the Caribbean, there were fewer soldiers in the region. According to author Charles Johnson, "They entered the harbor of Trespassy [in Newfoundland] with their black colors flying, drums beating and trumpets sounding. There were two-and-twenty vessels in the harbor which the men all quitted upon the sight of the pirate and fled ashore."[1]

Roberts seemed fearless. The pirates' crimes were being written about in his home country of England and in the colonies. *The Boston Newsletter* reported that, "The first thing the pirates did was to strip both passengers and seamen of all their money and clothes which they had on board, with a loaded pistol to everyone's breast, ready to kill anyone who resisted."[2]

The accounts of Robert's havoc were probably exaggerated. *The Boston Newsletter* published the bloodiest stories told by people who claimed to have been there. Their tales of horror were impossible to prove. There were claims that Roberts and his men killed a number of fishermen.

In the early 1700s, most pirate attacks occurred in warm waters near South America and the Caribbean. During the summer of 1720, Roberts and his men attacked ships off the coast of Newfoundland, a cold and undeveloped part of Canada.

There is little evidence that it happened in fact. The sailors who were robbed by Roberts often made the attacks sound worse than they really were. They did so because they didn't want people to believe they had given up without a fight.

Fortune's Plunder

In September 1720, the weather grew colder. Roberts and his crew headed back south. They had a new ship, the *Fortune*, which was loaded with 26 guns. In the Caribbean, Roberts was featured in more news stories claiming he and his pirates were brutal killers. Like the stories from Newfoundland, there were few facts to support them.

Beginning with the small hauls in Newfoundland, Roberts enjoyed an unbroken string of purchases. He overtook a number of ships along the Eastern Caribbean. His greatest success took place near the island of Martinique.

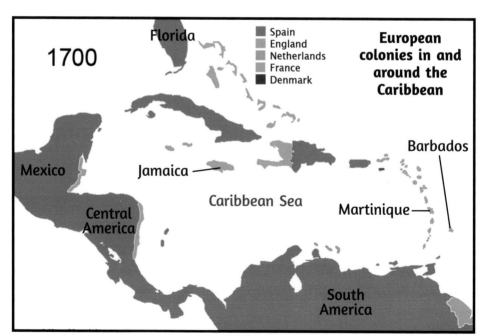

Roberts' most successful attacks occurred in the waters surrounding the European colonies of the Caribbean.

Yet this was also the site of some of the bloodiest tales of his piracy.

Commanding two large ships, Roberts sailed into the French **colony** with some 150 men under his command. The 52 cannons on board discouraged all but the bravest from fighting them.

Roberts did not attack the ports along Martinique. The island had too many forts and too many well-trained soldiers. Instead, he relied on the fact that the locals were unhappy with a law that had been imposed by the French. The French forbade trading with the Dutch, hoping to keep the money in their own country. Instead of entering the Martinique port, a Dutch ship would fly her flag and then go to nearby Dominica to wait. Soon enough, traders reached the ships laden with goods they hoped to sell, or money they planned to use to buy from the Dutch.

Roberts's ship had a brand new flag, which showed him standing astride a pair of skulls. He chose not to fly it. Instead as he sailed around Martinique, he gave merchants a familiar signal. He raised the Dutch flag. Then he sailed into the cove and waited. In a very short time, Roberts had taken over fifteen ships. For nearly a year, he and his men had avoided battles.

The pirate's luck changed within a year. On January 18, 1721, a real Dutch ship crossed their path. A slaver from Africa, the 300-ton vessel displayed nearly two dozen guns. The fight was brutal, but the pirates prevailed.

Despite the Dutch loss of life, it's unlikely the battle resembled the bloodbath described by Bermuda's governor, Benjamin Bennet, who said, "What men the pirates found alive on board they put to death. . . . Some were almost whipped to death, others had their ears cut off. An unlucky few were tied up and used as target practice.[3]

There is little evidence for this account. During this time, stories told secondhand also claim Roberts' men hanged the governor of Martinique. There is more evidence that he and his men set fire to a ship, which sank with some 80 slaves still trapped in the cargo hold. Clearly, Roberts was not the perfect pirate hero who took the bounty from rich shipping vessels and gave it to his poor crew. Neither was he the savage killer some made him out to be.

In any event, a mean reputation—even an untrue one— is a good thing for a pirate. It meant ships were more willing to surrender without a fight. When Roberts flew his colors, no one wanted to become another one of his victims. Unfortunately, his increasingly horrifying reputation meant that the navies of Europe grew even more interested in killing Black Bart.

Defended by Fort Royal, Martinique was protected from pirate attacks. Rigid trading rules were the island's undoing as merchants left its safety for the open water. Roberts and his pirate crew took advantage of the opportunity, quickly robbing over a dozen ships.

What's in a Name

Sometime, midway through his career as a pirate, John Roberts began going by the name Bartholomew. Like many pirates, he probably took on a new name to hide his identity. He also may have wanted to honor Bartholomew Sharp, a privateer and pirate who terrorized the seas in the 1600s.

In most books about the pirate John Roberts, the nickname "Black Bart" is often used. Although this is the name he is known by today, it was not what he was called during his lifetime. Indeed, the first person to call Roberts "Black Bart" was neither a fellow pirate nor a victim. It was a poet.

Like Roberts, Isaac Daniel Hooson was born in Wales. He was an attorney who became a successful poet near the end of his life. One of his best known poems was called "Black Bart." Later set to music, the poem described Roberts as a hero for only attacking British ships. Of course, in real life, the pirate worried less about a ship's country of origin than the value of her cargo.

Hooson probably called him "Black Bart" because of his skin color—in the early twentieth century, darker-skinned people from Ireland and Wales were often called "Black Irish" or "Black Welsh." Today, the name is often used to describe the calm way he attacked and killed other sailors, as though Roberts' heart, and not his skin, was "black."

The well-born son of an English lawyer, Sir Chaloner Ogle commanded the HMS Swallow. Charged with ending the piracy of Bartholomew Roberts and defending the West African coast against pirate attacks, his victory would earn him a knighthood.

Modern Books About Centuries-Old Stories

In writing a biography of John "Bartholomew" Roberts, an author examines as many sources as possible about the subject. The author must make a judgment about the reliability of Charles Johnson's work. There are a number of reasons many modern biographers choose to quote Johnson.

First, it must be taken into account that in the present day, major newspapers are generally considered to be a reliable source of information. During the time of Roberts and Johnson, papers often made up their stories. They would begin with the true account of someone robbed by a pirate like Roberts. Then they would add details, because the more frightening the account, the more readers the newspaper would attract. Reading about pirates was a popular entertainment in the early 1700s. Many papers were sold because readers were seeking these kinds of stories.

When writing a biography of a person who lived hundreds of years ago, diaries and other writings by the people who lived at the time are also important. Although there are no such writings linked to Roberts, accounts of his actions have been recorded by the captains and crew members of the ships he robbed. Unfortunately, these accounts were often exaggerated. Captains could face punishment if they did not show strong enough resistance to pirates. Given these circumstances, the works by Johnson are a valuable source for authors, since he interviewed a number of crew members who served with Roberts.

A GENERAL
HISTORY
OF THE
PYRATES,
FROM
Their first Rise and Settlement in the Island of Providence, to the present Time.

With the remarkable Actions and Adventures of the two Female Pyrates
MARY READ and ANNE BONNY;

Contain'd in the following Chapters,

Introduction.
Chap. I. Of Capt. Avery.
II. Of Capt. Martel.
III. Of Capt. Teach.
IV. Of Capt. Bonnet.
V. Of Capt. England.
VI. Of Capt. Vane.
VII. Of Capt. Rackam.
VIII. Of Capt. Davis.

IX. Of Capt. Roberts.
X. Of Capt. Worley.
XI. Of Capt. Lowther.
XII. Of Capt. Low.
XIII. Of Capt. Evans.
XIV. Of Capt. Phillips.
XV. Of Capt. Spriggs.
XVI. Of Capt. Smith.
And their several Crews.

To which is added,
A short ABSTRACT of the Statute and Civil Law, in Relation to Pyracy.

The Second Edition, with considerable Additions.

By Captain CHARLES JOHNSON.

LONDON:
Printed for, and sold by T. Warner, at the Black-Boy in Pater-noster-Row, 1724.

Bartholomew "Black Bart" Roberts terrorized Caribbean shipping lanes in the early 1700s. Today his statue looks out over the island of St. Thomas.

Historical Fact or Legend?

John Roberts was one of the most successful pirates in the world. In just two years, he and his crew seized over 400 ships. According to most accounts, he only got into serious battles with a small number of ships. This gives greater substance to the stories about him, affirming that they are more fact than legend.

The large number of ships that Roberts seized indicates that there were many witnesses. In a good number of cases, these men made the attacks seem worse than they were. Taking all of this into account, one gets an idea of his tactics and the number of times Roberts boarded and plundered ships.

Surprisingly, some of the most reliable accounts of Roberts' attacks come from his fellow pirates. Often they had little to gain by lying. After they were sentenced to death, they gave final statements about what they had done. These men who sailed beside Roberts provide the best account we have of this man who preferred tea to rum, and early bedtimes to late nights. A quote attributed to Roberts after his death provides a final image and summary of the glory of piracy:

"In honest service there is . . . low wages and hard labor; in this [piracy], plenty and satiety, pleasure and ease, liberty and power . . . a merry life and a short one shall be by motto." In this, Roberts got his wish.[1]

Chapter Notes

Chapter 1. Death of a Pirate

1. Charles Johnson,"Of Captain Bartholomew Roberts and His Crew," *A General History of the Robberies and Murders of the Most Notorious Pyrates*. London: Rivington, 1724; reprint, New York: Dodd, Mead, 1926; Books on Demand, 2009, p.176

2. Charles Johnson, "Foreword," *Pirates* (by C. Lovat Fraser). London: Rivington, 1735; reprint New York: R.M. McBride, 1922, p. x.

Chapter 2. Life at Sea

1. Charles Johnson,"Of Captain Bartholomew Roberts and His Crew," *A General History of the Robberies and Murders of the Most Notorious Pyrates*. London: Rivington, 1724; reprint, New York: Dodd, Mead, 1926; Books on Demand, 2009, p. 211.

Chapter 3. The Reluctant Pirate

1. Richard Sanders, "Prologue." *If A Pirate I Must Be: The True Story of 'Black Bart,' King of the Caribbean Pirates*. New York: Skyhorse Publishers, 2007, p. 12.

2. Charles Johnson, "Of Captain Bartholomew Roberts and His Crew," *A General History of the Robberies and Murders of the Most Notorious Pyrates*. London: Rivington, 1724; reprint, New York: Dodd, Mead, 1926; Books on Demand, 2009, p. 168.

3. Ibid., p. 182.

4. Ibid., p. 184.

Chapter Notes

Chapter 4. Some Good Plunders

1. Charles Johnson,"Of Captain Bartholomew Roberts and His Crew," *A General History of the Robberies and Murders of the Most Notorious Pyrates*. London: Rivington, 1724; reprint, New York: Dodd, Mead, 1926; Books on Demand, 2009, p. 187.

2. Richard Sanders, "Fishers of Men" *If A Pirate I Must Be: The True Story of 'Black Bart,' King of the Caribbean Pirates*. New York: Skyhorse Publishers, 2007, p. 113.

3. Ibid., "The Great Pirate Roberts," p. 148.

Chapter 6. Historical Fact or Legend?

1. Richard Sanders, "Postscript," *If A Pirate I Must Be: The True Story of 'Black Bart,' King of the Caribbean Pirates*. New York: Skyhorse Publishers, 2007, p. 248.

Works Consulted

Books

Burgess, Douglas R. *The Pirates' Pact: the Secret Alliances between History's Most Notorious Buccaneers and Colonial America*. Chicago: McGraw-Hill, 2008.

Johnson, Charles. *A General History of the Robberies and Murders of the Most Notorious Pirates*. London: Rivington, 1724; reprint, New York: Dodd, Mead, 1926; Books on Demand, 2009.

Johnson, Charles. *Pirates* (by C. Lovat Fraser) London: Rivington, 1735; reprint New York: R.M. McBride, 1922.

Konstam, Angus. *The History of Pirates*. New York: Lyons Press, 1999.

Konstam, Angus, and Roger Kean. *Pirates: Predators of the Seas*. New York: Skyhorse Publishers, 2007.

Lewis, Jon E. *The Mammoth Book of Pirates*. New York: Carroll & Graf Publishers, 2006.

Little, Benerson. *How History's Greatest Pirates Pillaged, Plundered, and Got Away With It: The Stories, Techniques, and Tactics of the most Feared Sea Rovers from 1500–1800*. Beverly, Massachusetts: Fair Winds Press, 2011.

Sanders. Richard. *If A Pirate I Must Be: The True Story of 'Black Bart,' King of the Caribbean Pirates*. New York: Skyhorse Publishers, 2007.

Woodard, Colin. *The Republic of Pirates: Being the True and Surprising Story of the Caribbean Pirates and the Man who Brought Them Down*. Orlando: Harcourt, 2007.

Periodicals

Sanders, Richard. "Hello, Sailor! The Real Pirate of the Caribbean," *Spectator*. June 23, 2007. Biography in Context. Web. June 12, 2014.

Further Reading

Chrisp, Peter. *Pirates*. New York: Kingfisher, 2011. Print.

Konstam, Angus, and David Rickman. *Pirate: the Golden Age*. Oxford: Osprey Publishers, 2011.

Platt, Richard, and Steve Stone. *Pirates vs Pirates*. London: Kingfisher, 2010.

Temple, Bob. *The Golden Age of Pirates: An Interactive History Adventure*. Mankato, Minnesota: Capstone Press, 2008.

On the Internet

Charles Johnson
https://archive.org/details/piratesjohn00johnrich
https://openlibrary.org/books/OL23301158M/A_General_History_of_the_Pyrates_from_Their_first_Rise_and_Settlement_in_the_Island_of_Providence_to

John Roberts
http://www.thewayofthepirates.com/famous-pirates/bartholomew-roberts.php

Pirate Game
http://www.bbc.co.uk/cbeebies/swashbuckle-online/games/swashbuckle-adventures/

St. Augustine Museum
http://www.piratesoul.com/index.php?option=com_content&view=article&id=94:black-bart&catid=46:notable-pirates&Itemid=199

Glossary

buccaneers (bu-ku-NEERs)—pirates who preyed on Spanish ships in the 1600s

colony (KOL-uh-nee)—people or land that is separated from a ruling power but is still governed by it

democracy (DEM-ah-krah-see)—rule by the people; people are allowed to vote for their leaders who make the laws

desert (DEH-sert)—leaving without planning to return, especially a military unit

empire (Em-PY-er)—a group of nations ruled over by a powerful leader like a king, queen or emperor

galleons (GAL-ee-uhn)—a large sailing ship in use from approximately the 1400-1600s

navigate (NAV-ih-gayt)—to direct the course of a ship

plantation (Plan-TAY-shun)—a large farm, especially one in the tropics, where cotton, sugar or coffee is usually grown

plundering (PLUHN-der-ing)—robbing goods or valuables by force

Index

About the
Author

Born in Boston, Massachusetts, John Bankston began writing articles while still a teenager. Since then, over two hundred of his articles have been published in magazines and newspapers across the country, including travel articles in *The Tallahassee Democrat*, *The Orlando Sentinel* and *The Tallahassean*. He is the author of over sixty biographies for young adults, including works on Alexander the Great, scientist Stephen Hawking, author F. Scott Fitzgerald, and actress Jodie Foster.